COLORADO

I n 1981, my parents had just moved from the east coast to Colorado and I visited them and the state for the first time. Sitting in their kitchen in Lakewood on the first morning, I was distracted by the view out the window looking west toward the seemingly nearby, purple mountains. The Rockies looked nearby because they are massive.

That same day we drove up into the mountains west of Denver on Interstate 70 as far as Georgetown where we viewed mountain goats scampering high up on the peaks surrounding that town. This highway is an astounding feat of engineering. At every bend there is a grand vista of color and shapes. Since that first encounter, I have had the pleasure of returning to Colorado a number of times and seeing many of the wonders in the state.

Colorado appeals to a wide range of people because it contains a wide range of climates, unique geographic elements, and a grand history. The very name of the state, deriving from Spanish and meaning red-colored, alludes to Colorado's colorful palette. Whether you come to ski, to hike in and climb the mountains, to ride the rapids or fish in the rivers, to see natural wonders, or to explore old and mysterious civilizations, you're bound to see more than you expect.

The Great Plains, pancake-flat with fields of wheat, slope upwards and cover the eastern part of the state. By the time they get to Denver they are a mile above sea level. The Rocky Mountains' snow-capped towering peaks form the state's spine running north-south. West of the Rockies lies a dry, wind-swept desert. In the south, there is abundant evidence of old Native American civilizations, as well as the legacy of the 16th century Spanish explorers.

Colorado has a myriad of unique features—from the country's highest town, highest railroad, highest paved road, and highest suspension bridge to fantastic gorges, 55 peaks over 14,000 feet, hot springs, and some of the sweetest peaches grown anywhere in the world. Wherever you find yourself in Colorado, you are not far from some wonder.

Colorado's mountains have always been the state's chief draw. Along U.S. Highway 24, between Salida and Leadville, the Fourteeners of the Sawatch Range stand like mighty guards. Mightiest of them all is Mount Elbert, the second tallest peak in the United States. Colorado mountains first attracted fur trappers and later the gold and silver miners. Today, gigantic tracks of Colorado land have been set aside as national parks and forests, wilderness and recreation areas. A few hours drive from Denver brings you to the magical mountain scenery of Rocky Mountain National Park, or to the fantastic rock formations of the Garden of the Gods, or to the ski meccas of Summit County.

In Colorado, you will have to stop and decide what to do. See ghost towns? Take the time to drive or bicycle one of the unsurpassed scenic highways? Visit one of hundreds of remote mountain lakes? Maybe see wildlife in Rocky Mountain National Park? Set out on a honest-to-goodness wilderness experience?

The collection of photos in this book focuses on the natural beauty of Colorado. But Colorado lacks nothing in cultural opportunities. You can spend your morning skiing in Aspen and end your day with a little Mozart. There are top museums of every sort, also dance, theater, music and prestigious film festivals all over the state.

In putting this book together, I looked at thousands of photos by talented photographers. Talk about an embarrassment of riches! With finite space, not everything could be included. And as amazing as these photographs are, the reality of Colorado is even greater—it's awesome! Surely, most visitors to Colorado would agree that the colors and vistas of the photos in this volume are representative of the very things they have witnessed personally.

BELOW: The Sneffels Range in the San Juan Mountain.

NEXT PAGE: Rock formations in Garden of the Gods make a spectacular frame for Pikes Peak.

O beautiful for spacious skies
For amber waves of grain
For purple mountain majesties
Above the fruited plain!

America the Beautiful, 1913, Katherine Lee Bates

Katherine Lee Bates wrote *America the Beautiful* after a visit to Pikes Peak.
She said she felt great joy when she saw the view.
"All the wonder of America seemed displayed there, with the sea-like expanse."

Denver was born during the great *Pikes Peak or Bust* Gold Rush of 1859 when flakes of placer gold were found at the confluence of the South Platte River and Cherry Creek. In its first years, Denver survived a flood, two major fires, and several Indian attacks. With the discovery of more gold in the mountains, Denver became a boomtown and ultimately became the Mile High City.

It is a clean, young, and green city with over 200 parks. It is a fast-growing city, having more than doubled its population since 1960. It is situated 15 miles east of the foothills of the Rockies. The wind blowing down from the Rockies gains heat as it descends and can bring 60° F weather to Denver at any time throughout the winter. In summer, low relative humidity makes Denver feel cool and comfortable.

Denver has a central downtown area. Here, within walking distance, are hotels, the city's convention complex, performing arts complex, and a wide variety of shops, restaurants, and nightspots. Also within walking distance are some of the city's top attractions including the U.S. Mint, Denver Art Museum, and Colorado History Museum. A mile-long pedestrian mall cuts through the heart of downtown Denver, with a series of parks and plazas that soften the towering skyscrapers and provide vantage points from which to appreciate the modern architecture.

With an average 300 days of sunshine a year, Denver is a sports capital. In addition to the Broncos, Nuggets, Avalanche, and Rockies, there is every kind of participatory-sport opportunity available. The city offers 400 miles of bike paths, over 70 local golf courses, and over 140 free tennis courts. Hiking, river rafting, climbing, and world-class ski resorts are all nearby.

Denver is indeed perfectly located as a starting place to explore the myriad of Colorado's attractions. It is also, in itself, a wonderful destination.

BELOW: The Colorado State Capitol was designed by E.E. Myers and was completed in 1908. It stands a mile above sea level with a plaque on the 15th step marking the spot that is 5,280 feet high. The dome is covered with 200 ounces of pure gold, and there is a beautiful view from the Rotunda of the entire Front Range. The interior of the capitol is built with the rare Colorado Rose Onyx (aka Beulah Red marble). The entire known supply of that stone was used up in the process.

AT RIGHT: The skyline of Denver has grown steadily since the end of World War II, but it was in the 1980s that Denver experienced a huge skyscraper building boom.

TOP: With its 370 acres, City Park hosts such attractions as the Denver Zoo, the IMAX Theatre, City Park Golf Course, and the Museum of Nature and Science. This view of the Front Range of the Rocky Mountains which Denver enjoys is tinged with sunrise colors.

LEFT: Coors Field, home to the Colorado Rockies, opened April 9, 1993 to the largest audience ever to attend an opening game. Fans sitting along first base and right field are treated to spectacular views of the Rockies. Most of the seats are green, but the upper deck's 20th row is painted purple, symbolizing the fact that here the seats are exactly one mile above sea level.

ABOVE: Denver International Airport is one of the world's busiest airports. The 1.4 million square foot main terminal building is one of Denver's most distinctive architectural landmarks. The roof is Teflon-coated fabric shaped into 32 peaks, symbolizing the Rocky Mountains. Fortunately, it is one of the most efficient airports and frequently ranks near the top on lists of airports with the least delays.

OPPOSITE: Every January, Denver hosts the granddaddy of rodeos, the Western Stock Show, Rodeo & Horse Show. It is a prestigious event for professional cowboys who bring excitement to the stands, riding bareback on twisting and bucking broncos and ferocious bulls.

TOP LEFT: Golden, Colorado, west of Denver was, for a time, the capital of Colorado. It is home to the Coors Brewing Company (at center of photo). Established in 1873, it is the world's largest single-site brewery.

MIDDLE LEFT: Larimer Square in downtown Denver has been restored to its 19th century charm and is a vibrant shopping, dining, and entertainment center.

TOP RIGHT: The Pepsi Center anchors the Lower Downtown district (LODO). It opened in 1999 and is home to the Denver Nuggets and the Colorado Avalanche. It also hosts numerous concerts.

MIDDLE RIGHT: The 16th Street Pedestrian Mall in the heart of downtown Denver features shops, cafés, and affords great people-watching. A free shuttle bus runs the length of the mall.

BOTTOM: Invesco Field at Mile High opened in 2001 and is home to the Denver Broncos. State-of-the-art technology was combined with the desire to maintain the intimacy for which the old Mile High Stadium had been famous.

Located 35 miles northwest of Downtown Denver, Boulder sits in the Boulder Valley where the Rocky Mountains meet the Great Plains. The year 1876 brought the admission of Colorado into the Union and with statehood, a state provision was passed establishing the University of Colorado at Boulder. Boulder has been called "the little town nestled between the mountains and reality," a saying referring to the quality of life enjoyed by residents and visitors alike. It is a captivating mountain community enriched with a natural beauty and diverse cultural opportunities. Its population of over 90,000 people includes the 25,000 students annually at the university. It supports a rich cultural scene with over 30 art galleries, two museums, 32 movie and stage theaters, and many festivals.

Boulder residents embrace the outdoor lifestyle. Early in the town's history a buffer zone around the city was created to maintain the surrounding natural beauty. There are over 200 miles of hiking and biking paths, and about 30,000 acres of open space, including the 16-mile Boulder Creek Path which runs through the middle of town.

TOP: Aerial view of Boulder showing the sheer cliffs of nearby El Dorado Springs, a haven for rock climbers. Boulder is also home to the University of Colorado, one of the largest schools in the state.

LEFT: The iconic Flatirons of Boulder are of Fountain-Formation sandstone that crops out along the Front Range in Colorado. The Garden of the Gods, near Colorado Springs, are of the same origin. The stone is reddish because of the presence of abundant pink fledspar grains within it. It was deposited about 290 million years ago. Adjacent to the Flatirons is the National Center for Atmospheric Research, established in 1960 to study climactic changes and atmospheric chemistry.

ROCKY MOUNTAIN NATIONAL PARK

Established in 1916, Rocky Mountain National Park preserves 265,000 acres of spectacular mountain scenery. The park boasts 150 pristine lakes, 350 miles of trails, and the largest concentration of wildlife in the southern Rocky Mountains. More than 60 peaks exceed 12,000 feet above sea level. The distinct, blocky summit of Longs Peak towers above them all at 14, 259 ft.

Straddling the Continental Divide, Rocky Mountain National Park contains the headwaters of the Colorado River. One-third of the park lies above treeline at 11,500 feet. This alpine tundra, or land above the trees is accessible by Trail Ridge Road, the highest paved continuous highway in the United States.

Beginning at 8,000 feet in open meadows of ponderosa pine and Douglas fir, Trail Ridge Road winds upward into cool dense forests of spruce and fir graced with exquisite wildflower gardens. Climbing higher, constant gusts batter and twist the trees into grotesque shapes. By 11,000 feet, frigid temperature, wind, and aridity stunt and eventually stop tree growth altogether. At 11,500, the road emerges into an arctic-like world above the trees where wildflowers carpet the rolling landscape. Trail Ridge Road traverses the same pathways that native people used to cross the Rocky Mountains for thousands of years.

BELOW: Elk *(Cervus elaphus)* or Wapiti—the Shawnee name meaning white deer—are commonly seen throughout Rocky Mountain National Park. Only the males have antlers, which are shed each winter. Large racks, growing up to 5 feet across, are used to fight for the right to mate the females, or cows, in the spectacular autumn mating ritual.

OPPOSITE: "Rock Cut" was blasted to allow passage of Trail Ridge Road, creating a window-frame view of fresh snow on the cliffs above Forest Canyon. In the distance, the distinct blocky-topped summit of Longs Peak reigns 14,259 feet above sea level.

Morning sun delicately illuminates Big Thompson Creek in Moraine Park. The broad valley, or park, was carved by ice-age glaciers. The Moraine is the tree-clad ridge of rocky debris left behind from the glaciers' retreat. The Big Thompson Creek is a favorite among anglers. With headwaters high in Forest Canyon, it meanders through Moraine Park before giving way to spectacular rapids.

ABOVE: Sprague Lake below Hallett Peak (elevation 12,713 feet). Albert Sprague homesteaded here more than a century ago and opened Sprague Lodge. In order to improve the quality of fishing for his guests, he built a small dam which enlarged the lake to its present 10.6-acre size.

AT RIGHT: Snow-covered trees below Hallett Peak as viewed from Storm Pass Trail. Winter comes early to the high elevations of Rocky Mountain National Park. There is plenty of snow west of the Continental Divide by November, slightly later on the drier, eastern slopes. The enormous amount of snow that falls annually in the Rockies has widespread impact. The Colorado River, which has its headwaters in Rocky Mountain National Park, flows 1,470 miles to the Gulf of California (sea of Cortez). It provides water for the growing populations of Arizona, California, and New Mexico.

OPPOSITE: Rocky Mountain National Park is home to more than 1,000 flowering plants. Alpine flowers are small and hug the ground, an adaptation to avoid the wind which robs plants of precious heat and moisture. The cluster of star-shaped stonecrop blooms bright yellow on the alpine tundra. Its succulent stems contain anthocyanin—a red pigment that converts sunlight to heat—another adaptation to survive the harsh alpine climate.

ABOVE: Trail Ridge Road was the first auto highway to cross the Continental Divide in northern Colorado. Eleven miles ribbon above treeline with a high point 12,183 feet, connecting the towns of Estes Park and Grand Lake. Overlooks, self-guided trails, and the Alpine Visitor Center provide opportunities to experience and learn more about Colorado's highest ecosystem, the alpine tundra. Trail Ridge Road is usually open from Memorial Day to mid-October. In winter, it is impassable not only due to snow, but to huge snowdrifts that accumulate in winds frequently over 100 miles per hour. The Continental Divide runs from British Columbia to Mexico. All water flows either east or west from this crest.

Humans began to venture into the area now known as Rocky Mountain National Park about 11,000 years ago after the last Ice Age. The lush valleys, alpine meadows, and crystal-clear lakes became favorite hunting grounds for the Ute and Arapaho people through the mid-1800's.

ABOVE RIGHT: Seemingly stark at first glance, the alpine tundra supports a variety of plants and animals that have adapted to frigid temperatures and constant wind in this arctic-like environment. Yellow-bellied marmots are often seen sunning on rocks in between bouts of eating as they prepare for winter hibernation. Mule deer are also seen grazing along the road. The high altitude ecosystem is fragile. Some alpine plants take 100 years to grow an inch!

OPPOSITE: Fall-colored grasses surround this beaver pond along Glacier Gorge. Beavers often dam streams to form ponds, a safe haven from predators. They build their lodges of aspen, willow, and sod. A beaver's ability to alter a landscape is second only to that of humans.

n the 1950s, the United States government under President Dwight Eisenhower, began in earnest to build the Interstate Highway System. Interstate 70 traverses 451 miles as it goes east–west across Colorado. The construction of Interstate 70 through the mountains of Colorado proved to be a decades-long battle for the engineers. It was not until 1993 that the final aspects of I-70 west of Denver were completed. The stretch from Denver through Glenwood Canyon is an absolute engineering marvel.

The two most noteworthy accomplishments are the Eisenhower Memorial Tunnel and the passage of the highway through Glenwood Canyon. The Eisenhower Tunnel opened in 1973 at a cost of $108 million. At the height of activity, as many as 1,140 workers were employed in three shifts, 24 hours a day, six days a week. It is the highest vehicular tunnel in the world, with an average elevation of 11,112 feet. Of the two tunnels, the eastbound is slightly longer at 1.697 miles.

The portion of the highway through Glenwood Canyon is no less spectacular. Some say it is an interstate where no interstate could ever go. Tiered, cantilevered bridges that carry westbound lanes atop

eastbound lanes were the elegant solution. Functional and attractive, the final stretch of I-70 cost hundreds of millions of dollars and is the most expensive stretch of interstate to date.

Along the way at numerous points, the views are wonderful. Slipping past shear mountain walls, graced by rivers with which it keeps company, rounding bends into wide valleys, it is a roller coaster of a road and a pleasure to ride, in and of itself. Add to that its virtue in making it easy to get up into the Rockies in all seasons. Along the way are many of Colorado's best recreational and historic attractions. Hiking, biking, river rafting, camping, skiing, and fishing are all available—to name only the more strenuous activities.

TOP RIGHT: Idaho Springs, Bridal Veil Falls. At its base is the largest water wheel in Colorado, built by goldminer Charlie Tayler who credited his good health to never shaving, bathing, or kissing a woman.

MIDDLE RIGHT: Wildlife around Mount Evans includes the Mountain goat (*Oreamnos americanus*). The mountain goat is not a true goat, but belongs to a group known as goat-antelopes. Its horns are nearly smooth and its hooves are well-adapted for gripping the steep surfaces.

BOTTOM RIGHT: River rafting opportunities abound in Colorado.

ABOVE: Red Rocks Amphitheater, a 10,000-seat natural outdoor theater just west of Denver.

BOTTOM LEFT: Mount Evans (elevation 14,254 feet) and Echo Lake. Mount Evans dominates the skyline west of Denver. The Mount Evans Scenic Byway starts near Idaho Springs and reaches the Summit of Mount Evans. This highest-paved road in the United States goes within a very short hike to the summit. (Trail Ridge Road in Rocky Mountain National Park is the highest paved *continuous* road in the United States.) This mountain and those nearby are dotted with mines from the 1860's Gold Rush.

TOP LEFT: Rock climbing is a popular activity in the mountains all along this route.

TOP RIGHT: Hanging Lake, Glenwood Canyon, is tucked away high on a ledge in a narrow canyon. The hike up to it is steep, but short. Bridal Veil Falls plunges into the north end of the lake. Schools of trout teem in the clear waters.

BELOW: Georgetown is nestled between some of the most majestic peaks in the state. Its fortunes rose and fell with the discovery of gold and the mining that ensued. Its Victorian charm is well-preserved.

ABOVE: Steam engines ran along the George Town Loop Railroad for over 30 years until it was retired by the Colorado Historical Society in 2004. This railroad icon representing Colorado's past carried passengers across Devil's Gate High Bridge at 95 feet above Clear Creek and passed the same spectacular mountain scenery visitors first saw at the run of the 19th century.

BOTTOM LEFT: Glenwood Hot Springs, the largest hot springs in the world, has been operating for over 100 years.

BOTTOM RIGHT: Lake Dillon is the largest water storage facility for the Denver metropolitan area. It was dammed in 1963 and is fed by the Blue River, Ten Mile Creek, and the Snake river. It offers world-class sailing in the heart of Summit County.

One hundred millions years ago the area around Grand Mesa was the swampy shore of an inland sea. Sediments settled into this soup and buried a large number of trees, ferns and other plants. Over geologic ages, this matter turned into coal. Above the coal, the tracks of dinosaurs can be found in the rocks. As time passed on, the sea disappeared and the area began to rise, producing a highly uneven surface. Later, extensive volcanic action produced immense amounts of lava filling in all the cracks and crevices and thus forming the flat surface that is the Grand Mesa of our geologic age.

During the last Ice Age, glaciers pushed across the top of the Mesa, leaving tracks called glacial striations, which can still be seen. The glaciers scooped out depressions that formed the Mesa's lakes. Grand Mesa has long dominated the landscape and the lives of people in the valleys below, providing food, water, shelter, and recreation. It is the world's largest flat-top mountain, with an average elevation of 10,000 feet and a summit rising to 11,000 feet. Evidence suggests that humans were living in the area about 10,000 years ago. It was used for hunting and fishing by the Ute tribe, who called it Thunder Mountain. The first Europeans to visit the area were members of the Dominquez-Escalante expedition of 1776 which crossed the Mesa led by Ute guides. Snowmelt on the Mesa fills over 300 alpine lakes and reservoirs.

BELOW: Grand Mesa National Forest, together with the Uncompahgre and Gunnison National Forests are a combination of separate National Forests on the western slope of the Rockies. These three combined forests cover 3,161,912 acres of public land. They vary in elevation from 5,800 feet in Roubideau Canyon to 14,309 feet on Uncompahgre Peak.

OPPOSITE: Mount Garfield is found east of Grand Junction. It rises to a height of 6,000 feet. Between Mount Garfield and Grand Mesa flows the Colorado River. Mount Garfield is the easternmost end of the Book Cliff mountain range which runs east–west into Utah.

COLORADO NATIONAL MONUMENT

Established in 1911 and comprised of about 32 square miles, Colorado National Monument preserves one of the grand landscapes of the American West. The spectacular Rim Rock Drive offers 23 miles of breath-taking panoramas with many overlooks from which to view canyons with sheer walls, towering monoliths, bighorn sheep, and soaring eagles. There are mountain lions among the wildlife living here as well.

The canyon bottoms have ancient Precambrian rocks covered by Triassic-age formations. Then come the Morrison Formations bearing dinosaur fossils. Three Cretaceous formations are exposed on top of the mesa at about 7,000 feet above sea level.

There are four main canyons cutting into the plateau for several miles, with several small ravines, isolated towers, and pinnacles, as well as other interesting rock formations. The cliffs are generally made of sandstone layers in various shades of red and white.

BELOW: The Coke Ovens are in Monument Canyon, the longest of the four main ravines that pierce the plateau. This canyon contains most of the major rock formations. The Coke Ovens, clearly visible from Rim Rock Drive, are at the end of a ridge which has eroded into a series of large, cream-colored mounds.

OPPOSITE: Independence Monument is an isolated 450 foot tower of sandstone at the junction of Monument and Wedding Canyons.

Spanish explorers came to Colorado as early as the 16th century in search of the fabled Cities of Gold. But it was the discovery of gold in California in 1849 that touched off the search for gold in the Rocky Mountains and accounted for the first extensive settlement of Colorado. In turn, William Russell's discovery of gold in present-day Denver touched off the *Pikes Peak or Bust* Gold Rush of 1858.

There are over 260 sites in Colorado which are considered ghost towns—ranging from unremarkable piles of rotten timber to quite-intact but abandoned towns. Some have bluntly-coined names such as Granite, Ironton, and Gold Hill. Other towns chose names reflecting the spirit of the undertaking, such as Bonanza, Climax, and Eureka. Sturdy, practical individuals as well as get-rich-quick dreamers flocked to wherever the latest discovery was made. Towns sprang up almost overnight. Fortunes were made by some and hopes were dashed for many.

BELOW: East of Marble, on the Crystal River, Dead Horse Mill powered a mechanical air compressor used in processing ore. Area silver mines kept Crystal going until the Silver Crash of 1893 nearly shut the town down. Subsequent mining efforts failed which doomed the town.

OPPOSITE TOP: The Independence Load was discovered July 4th, 1879, and soon after, a town of 300 sprang up. By 1882, there were 1,500 residents and over 40 businesses. With snow from October through May however, Independence (elevation 10,900 feet) did not last long.

OPPOSITE BOTTOM LEFT: Originally named Castle Forks and later Chloride, Ashcroft was founded in 1880 when gold was discovered in Castle Creek Valley. Three years later, there were 2,500 residents, two newspapers, a school, two sawmills, and 20 saloons. The mines soon played out. By 1900, there were only two people left.

OPPOSITE MIDDLE RIGHT: Less than four years after its start in 1879, Twin Forks had six hotels and had become a lavish resort for the carbonate kings of Leadville. Today it is a sleepy resort.

OPPOSITE BOTTOM RIGHT: Animas Forks once had a sign proclaiming itself the "largest city in the world," with small print saying "at this altitude" (elevation 11,300 feet). The first settlement dates to 1875. At least five mines extracted galena (lead ore) and silver-bearing grey copper. But, the town was plagued with avalanches. Snow would slide down one mountainside and up the other. Animas Forks had a lucrative period in the 1880s, but by the turn of the century output from the mines slowed and the mills shut down.

The San Juan Mountain Range, in southwestern Colorado, is considered by many to have the most beautiful and varied scenery in all of Colorado. Spanning the Continental Divide, the San Juans have numerous jagged volcanic summits, many lakes, waterfalls, and streams. It includes the sources of the Rio Grande River. The San Juans cover 12,000 square miles of southwestern Colorado, about one-eighth of the state.

These mountains are among the highest and most rugged in North America. They are relatively new, geologically speaking. Hundreds of peaks rise above 13,000 feet and thirteen rise above 14,000 feet. Sixty-five million years ago, the entire area was almost twice as high as it is today, although it was an elevated plateau and not a mountainous area. The present mountains arose about 35 million years ago in an extended period of volcanic activity. The Colorado Mineral Belt stretches northeast from the San Juans to Boulder. The San Juans are highly mineralized, and a great part of the gold and silver mining of Colorado took place in this region. The mountains are studded with excavation sites and old mining equipment clinging to the sides of mountains.

Much of the land is publicly owned. 1980 saw the creation of the Mount Sneffels Wilderness Area, located between Ouray and Telluride. Many of the best known sights are found close to the San Juan Skyway along Colorado 145 and U.S. 550. There are over 200 miles of dramatic, winding roads—with some precipitous drop-offs and curves for which one must slow down to as little as 10 miles per hour.

BELOW: The 14,150-foot peak on the left is Mount Sneffels, the jewel of the San Juan Range. In early fall the jagged mountain terrain is dusted with snow and the aspens have turned gold making a wonderful contrast. Mount Sneffels is a steep and beautiful mountain and typifies the San Juans in that it is surrounded by other enormous peaks.

Charles Baker entered this area in 1860 in search of gold dust in the sand and gravel bars of the Animas River. He did find some. And soon, hundreds—some say thousands—of prospectors were heading for the heart of San Juan country which was deep within Ute territory. By the end of 1861, all the prospectors had been driven out by disappointing results, harsh winters, and the hostile Utes. But in 1870 prospectors returned and legal arrangements were made with the Utes. Mines proliferated along the Animas, and railroad companies raced each other to reach the San Juans. The Denver and Rio Grande Railroad was first to roll from Durango into Baker's Park in 1882.

Silverton's history is typical of these mining towns, with many more men than women, lots of saloons, gambling, and houses of prostitution in designated red-light districts. In time, with the arrival of civilizing brides, propriety prevailed. Durango was created by the railroad builders who bought the land, laid out the city, and built their train yards and depots. The Durango and Silverton Narrow Gauge Railroad winds through canyons in the remote wilderness of San Juan National Forest. It first arrived in Durango in 1881 and was promoted as a scenic route for passengers. After weathering the difficult transition ensuing from the local decline in mining, the D&SNGR is polished and going strong.

Ouray, named after the famous Ute Chief Ouray, grew quickly with the coming of the Denver & Rio Grande in late 1887. Unlike many San Juan mining towns however, Ouray was, from the first, a tourist destination because of its spectacular location, relatively low elevation, and its hot springs.

BELOW: The Durango and Silverton Narrow Gauge Railroad is the oldest, continuously-operating narrow gauge line in the United States. Three miles below Needleton, the sound of the river and the wind is briefly interrupted by the sound of a steam-powered train, the *Silverton*.

ABOVE: Locomotive #481 pulls a heavy twelve-car train four miles south of Silverton.

LEFT: Nestled in a valley at 9,300 feet, the Victorian mining town of Silverton retains much of its gritty authenticity and frontier charm. Incorporated in 1876, Silverton's history is linked to the mineral riches of the surrounding mountains and was an active mining town until 1991 when the Sunnyside Mine closed.

OPPOSITE: Nicknamed the *Switzerland of America,* Ouray is renowned for its magnificent alpine mountains and stunning waterfalls such as this one in Box Canyon.

BELOW: The Cascade Canyon Winter Train, departing from Durango and traveling 26 miles to Cascade Canyon, provides a captivating five-hour round trip through the sparkling mountain landscapes and snow-covered wilderness of the San Juan Mountains.

For more than a millennium, various Indian cultures have lived, worked, and worshiped in the Four Corners area where Colorado, New Mexico, Arizona, and Utah come together. This highly-developed Indian culture-complex, called the Anasazi—Navajo for "ancient ones,"—were possibly ancestors of today's Hopi and Rio Grande Pueblo Indians. Their culture flourished between 500 and 1300 A.D. and appears to have come to an abrupt end.

One of the nation's largest archeological preserves, Mesa Verde National Park, was created in 1906 after a tireless campaign by the Colorado Federation of Women's Clubs to save the ruins from looters and destruction. Located ten miles east of Cortez off U.S. 160 where a score of deep canyons cut the mesa, the Park protects a particularly wonderful network of Anasazi ruins. In the shelter of hundreds of caves eroded high in the rocky walls are some of the largest and best-preserved Indian cliff dwellings in the world.

In the earlier phases of this culture, these people built subterranean pithouses on the mesa tops. Later in the 13th century, for reasons that are not entirely clear, they began to live in the caves and built complex cliff dwellings. It is known that a severe drought struck the area in 1276. It lasted for 24 years and certainly drove the Indians from their Mesa Verde dwellings to search for places to live with reliable water sources. Anasazi dwellings, ceramics and everyday objects show clearly that these were people who treasured beauty in everything around them.

A pair of six-mile loops, Ruins Road, affords views of over 35 cliff dwelling sites. There are carefully excavated and restored ruins throughout the Park which encompasses 125,000 acres of sandstone cliffs, green flat-topped plateaus, and deep, rugged canyons.

BELOW: The silent stone walls of Mesa Verde's ancient cliff dwellings tell the story of a civilization struggling to survive in a harsh environment. Once a prosperous and highly advanced Anasazi community, it was abandoned sometime before the close of the 13th century. Today, the remains of Mesa Verde are the best preserved ancient cliff dwellings in the United States and tell us much about their inhabitants culture and customs.

BLACK CANYON OF THE GUNNISON NATIONAL PARK

At the rate of about one inch every hundred years, the Gunnison River has scoured down through hard Precambrian rock to form the narrow, steep-sided Black Canyon. The high water volume of the river together with the high speed with which its water travels made this possible. It is incredibly deep, 2,722 feet at Warner Point. The Empire State Building, by comparison, is 1,250 feet tall. At the narrowest rim-to-rim point it is only 1,100 feet across. Its total length is 48 miles.

The rock layers of the Black Canyon tell a story of past environments and the processes which formed the various levels. It is believed that the present Gunnison River became established 10–11 million years ago. There had been enormous volcanic eruptions in the San Juan and the West Elk Mountain Ranges. This coincided with a period of uplift known to geologists as the Gunnison Uplift. The reasons for the uplifting of this large area are not well understood.

In the next two million years, the Gunnison had cut down through the lava layers to the basement rocks of the much harder Precambrian layers. The Gunnison no longer runs freely through the canyon. A series of three dams holds back the flood. In addition, water is brought by tunnel from the Gunnison to irrigate the Uncompahgre Valley to the south. The Gunnison Tunnel, begun in 1901 and finished in 1909, is eleven feet wide and twelve feet high, stretching almost six miles through hard rock, clay, sand, and shale. It is still in use today which is evident when one drives through the green Uncompahgre Valley.

BELOW AND NEXT PAGE: The views from the ridges in Black Canyon of the Gunnison National Park are breathtaking. It is possible to hike down into the canyon, though this trip is recommend only to the sturdy and sure-footed.

PAGE 33: The 20-mile-long Blue Mesa Lake is Colorado's largest body of water (covering 41,972 acres) and the largest Kakanee salmon fishery in the United States. Together with two other reservoirs, it forms the heart of Curecanti National Recreation Area.

PAGE 34: Mount Crested Butte is three miles north of Crested Butte, a popular skiing and mountain biking center. The area has been dubbed the Wildflower Capital of Colorado.

north America's tallest sand dunes rise over 700 feet high against the peaks of the Sangre de Cristo Mountains. Both Arizona and California have great sandy deserts, but they have nothing quite like the Great Sand Dunes of Colorado. Seeming oddly out of place next to the snow-covered Rocky Mountains in the San Luis Valley, these dunes cover an area of about 39 square miles. The flat, high San Luis Valley extends 100 miles south into New Mexico. It is bordered by the San Juan Mountains to the west and the Sangre de Cristo Mountains to the east.

The dunes were formed from sand deposited by the Rio Grande River and its tributaries that flow through the San Luis Valley. Prevailing westerlies have carried sand particles and deposited them at the east edge of the valley before rising to cross the Sangre de Cristo Mountains. This process has been going on for thousands of years and the dunes continue to grow by the same process today. These same westerlies change the shape of the dunes and continuously change the sand patterns of the dunes. This is a place where footprints are not a problem, unlike many desert parks of the Southwest where delicate sandy soil is easily damaged by visitors.

Though the dunes continually change shape, overall they maintain a remarkably stable form because they are quite moist throughout due to rain and snow. However, the surface layers of sand are dry and therefore flow with the wind.

Caution is advised for those exploring the dunes. Walking in sand dunes is strenuous. Shoes are a must since the surface temperature of the dunes can reach 140° F, much too hot for a dog's paws. Dramatic thunderstorms are common here in July and August. With lightning commonly striking the dunes.

BELOW: The Great Sand Dunes are a place to take a hike, observe animals and plants, to seek solitude, to take photographs, ride a horse, to camp in the wilderness, run, jump, or slide.

Emerging gradually from the plains of Kansas and Nebraska, the High Plains of Colorado slope gently upward for a distance of about 200 miles from the eastern border to the base of the foothills of the Rocky Mountains. They are generally level to rolling prairies, broken by occasional hills or bluffs. Elevations along the eastern border range from about 3,360 feet at its lowest point, where the Arkansas River crosses the border. Fully 41% of Colorado is taken up by these plains.

The old western heritage is etched deeply on the open spaces of these prairies. The history here is one of buffalo hunts, Spanish explorers in search of cities of gold, fur traders on the Sante Fe Trail, and cowboys driving their herds. In the northeast, cattle barons conquered the area in the 1860s and the area hasn't changed much since their time. Cowboys still saddle up and ride with the herd with eagles soaring overhead. These vast stretches are still as open as they were when the pioneers found them. The Homestead Act of 1862 attracted people here, promising them 160 acres of land on the provision that they live on that land and cultivate it for a period of years.

Colorado's High Plains are the easternmost extension of the Great Plains. Historically, this was the range of the bison and the Great Plains Culture of Cheyenne, Arapahoe and Comanche peoples.

BELOW: This view from a west-bound airplane gradually descending for landing in Denver presents this fascinating view that is reminiscent of an abstract painting. It is, of course, part of the vast agricultural activity carried out on the plains. With great variations in available water in the plains, both irrigated and "dry farming" are practiced. Major crops include wheat, spring grains, corn, alfalfa, and sugar beets. In the southern plains, many vegetables and melons are grown.

Spanning a quarter mile across the Royal Gorge is the world's highest suspension bridge, a marvelous engineering feat. It crosses the massive Royal Gorge and the raging Arkansas River. At 1,053 feet, views from the bridge are spectacular. Alongside this are two other marvels—the world's longest single-span Aerial Tram and the world's steepest Incline Railway. The Royal Gorge Route Railroad travels though twelve miles of unforgettable scenery on the most spectacular section of the Denver & Rio Grande Railroad directly through the Gorge.

The Gorge was created some three million years ago by the action of the Arkansas river, one of America's longest rivers. The river continues to cut through the granite rock at the rate of one foot every 2,500 years. At the canyon bottom, it is no more than 40–50 feet across. At the top. the gorge measures only a few hundred feet. Constructed in 1929, the bridge is extraordinarily strong, capable of supporting two million pounds.

Some of the earliest and largest dinosaurs roamed the area around the Gorge. Paleontologists have discovered several very nearly complete dinosaur remains less than three miles from Royal Gorge. Dating from 100 to 200 million years ago, fossil bones found here include the Altosaurus, Stegosaurus and Comtosaurus.

In 1877 silver was discovered on the upper Arkansas River. This sparked a controversy between two competing railroads, the Rio Grande and the Sante Fe, both wanted the rights to build the new freight lines to carry ore down from the mountain.

Known as the Royal Gorge War, the fighting consisted of exchanges of gun shots and of dynamiting competitor's building efforts. After a six-month court battle, the Santa Fe was unhappy with the results and hired legendary gun fighter Bat Masterson and some of his Kansas gang. The Rio Grande countered with a 200-man posse and The Rio Grande easily won.

LEFT: The Royal Gorge.

37

PIKES PEAK & GARDEN OF THE GODS

Towering to a height of 14,110 feet, Pikes Peak is located on the Front Range of the Rocky Mountains, fourteen miles west of Colorado Springs. It features the largest elevation gain of any mountain in Colorado, rising 7,800 vertical feet in 7.25 miles. Originally named Grand Peak, it was later renamed Pikes Peak shortly after it was encountered by Lt. Zebulon Montgomery Peak in 1806. The mountain was first ascended in 1820 by botanist Edwin James. By the mid-1800s, a trail to the top had been well established.

Pikes Peak's proximity to the edge of the Great Plains and its large size made it a frequent first sight for wagon trains coming west in search of fortunes and a new life, leading to the expression "Pikes Peak or Bust."

Since 1890, the Manitou and Pikes Peak Railway, the world's highest cog railway has taken passengers to the summit of Pikes Peak. The railway is 8.9 miles long and starts six miles from downtown Colorado Springs. From the summit on a clear day, it is possible to see the spires of Denver 70 miles away. It is also possible to drive to the summit on Pikes Peak Highway.

Much of the land that comprises Garden of the Gods was purchased in 1879 by railroad magnate Charles Perkins. After his death, the land was bequeathed to the city of Colorado Springs to be used as a park. It has long been recognized for its uncommon beauty and studied as a great archeological and geological treasure. As foreground to majestic Pikes Peak and backdrop to vast grasslands, Garden of the Gods houses plants and wildlife from both habitats in a remarkable mix of mountain and prairie dwellers—from bighorn sheep to prairie rattlesnake.

BELOW: Pikes Peak forms the dramatic background for Colorado Springs.

OPPOSITE TOP: A fleeting morning storm accentuates the beauty of these ancient monoliths of Garden of the Gods.

OPPOSITE BELOW: One of the most famous rocks in the country is Balanced Rock. This huge rock is balanced on a narrow support left when the surrounding area eroded away.

PAGE 40–41: Over millions of years, the extremes of ice and heat, wind and water have created nature's intricate and stunning artwork. When R.E. Cable visited this remarkable area in 1859, he exclaimed, "Why, this is a fit place for the gods to assemble a garden of the gods!"

PAGE 42–43: Thriving within Garden of the Gods is an abundance of plant and animal life. Pinyon pines and ancient junipers cover much of the dramatic landscape providing shelter and habitat for scrub jays, magpies, gray foxes, rabbits, squirrels, and many other types of animals.

Between Garden of the Gods and Pikes Peak, lies the magical town of Manitou Springs. Before the coming of the white man, the Ute, Cheyenne, and many other native peoples considered the area sacred. "Manitou" is a Native American word meaning "spirit." From oral traditions handed down from generation to generation, we learn that these people held the Earth to be sacred and believed that all living things have a soul which is part of the Great Spirit.

The Manitou Cliff Dwellings is a rare historical treasure. Built over 700 years ago, these Anasazi dwellings are protected by a red sandstone overhang. Earlier archeologists thought that the Anasazi disappeared without explanation, abandoning magnificent stone structures like the Cliff House and a half-million gallon reservoir at Mesa Verde. However, many clans of present-day Indian tribes trace their ancestry to the Anasazi. They say, "We are still here!"

There is strong scientific evidence suggesting that the Anasazi did not *mysteriously* disappear. Oral histories among the Hopi, Zuni, and Pueblo peoples, as well as scientific findings suggest that the exodus from the Anasazi culture centers may have been family-by-family or clan-by-clan and may have taken place over a hundred years. People moved and joined what are now Hopi and Zuni communities in Arizona and New Mexico along the Rio Grande.

Though it is not certain why the Anasazi left, it is very likely that a combination of forces were at work. For one thing, there were droughts. Tree-ring dating tells us that there was a 50-year drought from 1130 to 1180 A.D. and another from 1250 to 1300 A.D. In addition to the droughts, evidence points to a maurading enemy. The cliff dwellings themselves must have been highly defensible. Yet, if an enemy raided the agricultural fields and destroyed the remaining crops, the Anasazi might have fled to avoid starvation. Furthermore, some scientists suggest that things like poor sanitation, pests, and environmental degredation may have caused the Anasazi to move.

BELOW: The Manitou Springs Cliff Dwellings first opened to the public in 1906. Great care has been taken to preserve these structures. Yet, this is not a "hands-off" site. Visitors are allowed to enter the rooms to get a real sense of what life must have been like in the Anasazi world.

OPPOSITE: From June through August, traditional dancing, drumming, and singing are kept alive here in Manitou Springs. In Anasazi culture, dancing was important for more than its deep symbolic meaning and ritual purposes. The Anasazi had to be agile and to be able to maintain their balance on narrow cliff ledges or risk injury or death from a fall.

One hundred years ago, visitors to Cave of the Winds, located west of Colorado Springs, carried candles and lanterns along eerie, dark halls that seemed to have no end into mysterious chambers so large that the fragile lights they carried never reached the other side. Long before that, in 1000 A.D., the Jicarilla Apache lived here. They never went into the Cave, believing the moaning sound created by the winds in the Cave was the voice of the Great Spirit.

Seventy million years ago, the sea that had long covered this area receded. Seashells had accumulated here for millennia and had been compressed into limestone. As the earth pushed upward in mountain-forming activity, water mixed with carbon dioxide to form a weak carbonic acid and started to dissolve the limestone. Over thousands of years, this acid formed the caves. Then stalactites and other cave formations came to be as more of this acidic water continued to drip through the cave ceiling.

Nearby caves were discovered in the 1870s, but soon a couple of boys, John and George Pickett, found an overgrown trail leading to a hole in the mountain. They followed that trail and found the caves and tunnels that are now Cave of the Winds.

Located in a natural box canyon southwest of Colorado Springs, the Seven Falls cascade 181 feet in seven distinct steps down a solid cliff of Pikes Peak granite. The clear water from the southernmost edge of the Pikes Peak watershed have, over the ages, carved this unique scenic masterpiece. At the head of the cascades stand the Pillars of Hercules, mighty stone pillars on either side of the narrow gorge. Two hundred twenty-four steps along the side of the Falls lead to flower-decked banks. Spruce and pine trees line the canyon, adding to a striking scene of beauty.

BELOW: In the early 1900s, handrails, electric lights, and cement pathways were installed in the caves. Today, tours of various lengths are conducted year-round. Even on the hottest days, temperatures inside the Caves remain at about 54° F.

OPPOSITE: Nature may turn off the lights at night, but in the 1940s Albert Hill purchased the land around Seven Falls and added lighting which made it possible for spectators to enjoy the nighttime view. (Today's light show is far beyond that early installation.) Later, with the construction of the Eagle's Nest, an observation platform on the south wall of the canyon, all of the Seven Falls could be seen at once.

At the foot of the Rocky Mountains, the United States Air Force Academy is Colorado's most frequently visited man-made attraction. Its sleek modern architecture and its dramatic setting combine to create a stunning national institution. Its buildings of aluminum, steel, and glass are perfect reflections of the essential modernity of flying.

The architectural centerpiece of the Academy is the unique Cadet Chapel, a building which combines an utterly modern sensibility with elements that evoke a gothic cathedral. Its seventeen towering, triangular, parallel spires resemble a group of fighting jets pointing skyward.

Authorized by Congress in 1954, the Academy's first class assembled at Lowery Air Force Base in Denver. The permanent campus opened in 1958. The Air Force Academy was established during the first decade of the Cold War, when the threat of nuclear attack and Communist expansion loomed large. The Air Force Academy symbolized the importance of air power to United States security. As the Air Force became the nation's primary military arm during the 1950s, the Air Force Academy was charged with the training and education of officers capable of meeting the challenges of the Nuclear Age.

Approximately 4,000 cadets, both men and women, are enrolled in the four-year course that leads to a bachelor's degree and a position of second lieutenant. To be considered, applicants must obtain a nomination from the U.S. President or Vice President, a U.S. Senator. or a Member of the House of Representatives.

BELOW: A fighter jet mounted to suggest its powerful flight into the 'wild blue yonder,' together with the background setting of the Rockies' majestic Pikes Peak, makes a wonderful statement of the United States Air Force Academy's spirit.

OPPOSITE: U.S. Air Force Academy cadets celebrate their graduation in this time-honored tradition, while a formation of jets roars into sight overhead.

OPPOSITE, INSET: Massed like a phalanx of fighter jets shooting up into the sky, the Cadet Chapel, designed by Walter A. Nash, has become a symbol of the United States Air Force Academy. The interior provides three main worship areas, the Protestant Chapel, the Catholic Chapel, and the Jewish Chapel.

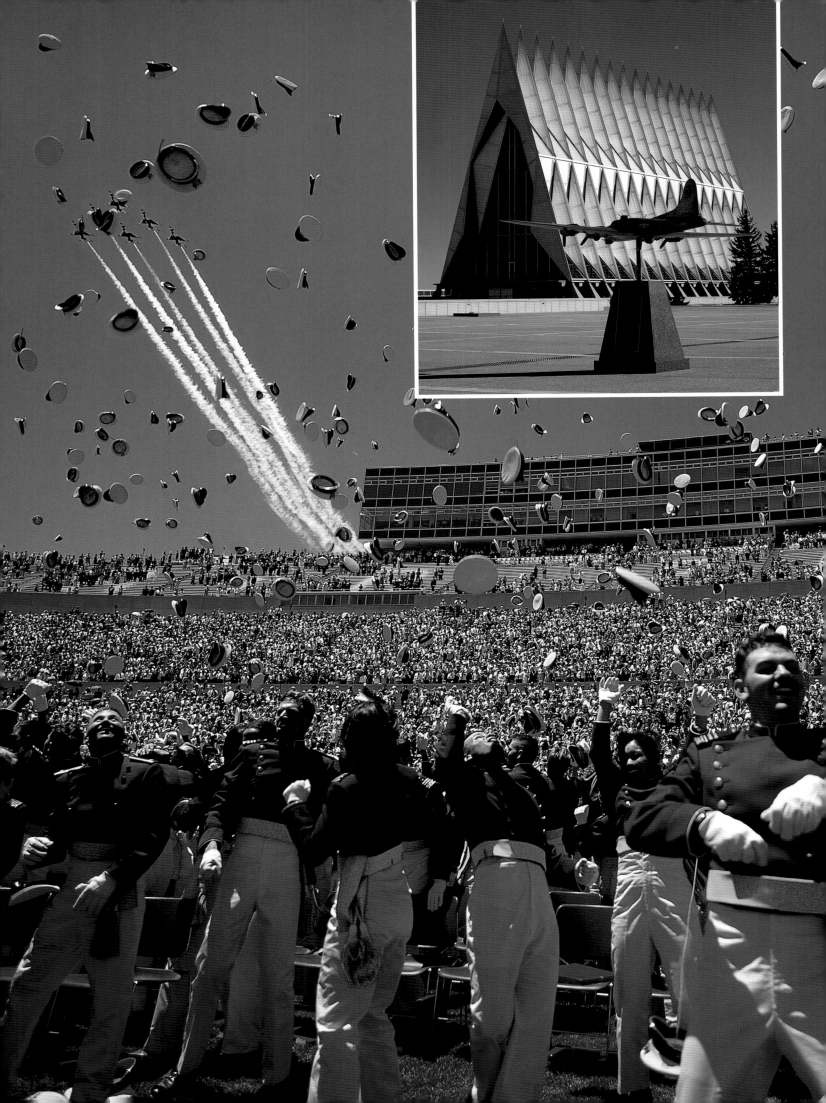

W hen it comes to skiing, no other state comes close to Colorado. In the heart of the Colorado Rocky Mountains, there is a multitude of opportunities for first-class skiing as well as every other type of winter snow activity. Colorado has what is known as "ski buzz." Here are America's highest and steepest ski mountains. Colorado has more skiable acres than any other state. Skiing is, however, far from all that is available in wintertime in the Rockies. Art, shopping, nightlife, festivals, fine dining, and hot springs add immeasurably to the appeal of Colorado's ski locales.

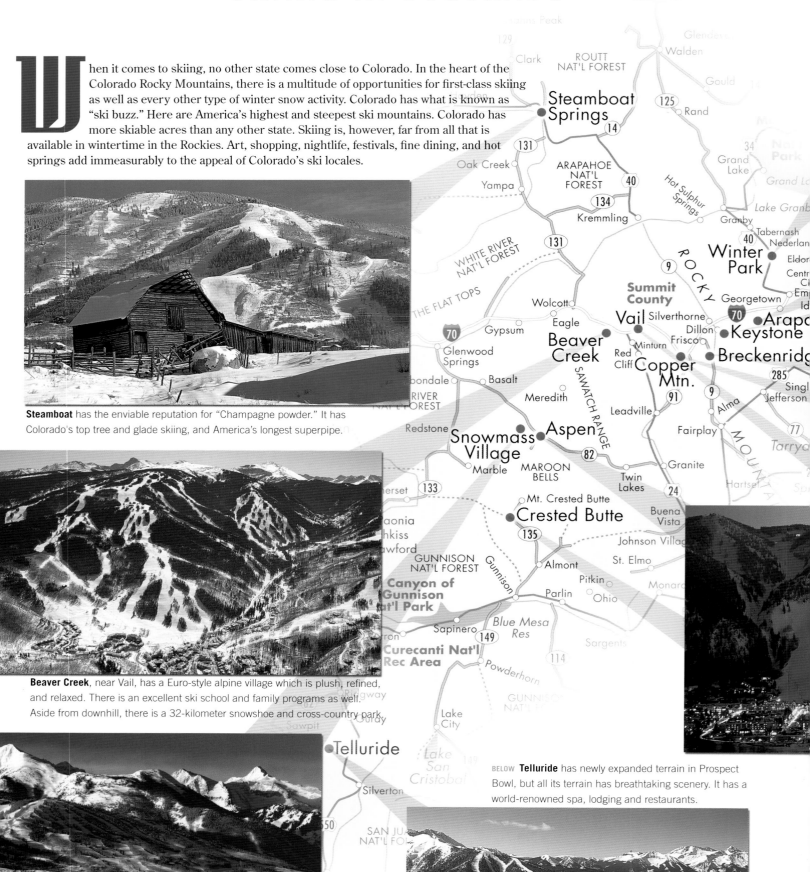

Steamboat has the enviable reputation for "Champagne powder." It has Colorado's top tree and glade skiing, and America's longest superpipe.

Beaver Creek, near Vail, has a Euro-style alpine village which is plush, refined, and relaxed. There is an excellent ski school and family programs as well. Aside from downhill, there is a 32-kilometer snowshoe and cross-country park.

BELOW **Telluride** has newly expanded terrain in Prospect Bowl, but all its terrain has breathtaking scenery. It has a world-renowned spa, lodging and restaurants.

Snowmass is Aspen's state-of-the-art venue, with the nation's longest lift-served vertical rise. It offers superior bowl and 95% of its lodging is ski-in–ski-out.

Winter Park is a five-mountain playground, offering extra-friendly family services. Its Mary Jane is renowned for bump-riding. It is, besides, the nation's largest center for disabled skiing.

Keystone, near Dillon, has three mountains and tons of extras: yoga, wine-tasting, ice skating, and kids' programs. It also has famous, gourmet restaurants.

Arapahoe Basin, near Keystone and Dillon, is America's highest ski terrain. It offers legendary steeps, a base-area "beach" with a party atmosphere. It attracts a lot of young people.

Breckenridge has a 140 year-old Victorian downtown and four mountains with varied terrain, suitable for all levels. It also has top-rated pipe and snowboard programs.

LEFT: With double-black diamond terrain, five-star service and sophistication, **Aspen** is rich in history and personality. It is also known for the high quality of its dining and nightlife. Skiing comes into the downtown.

RIGHT: **Copper Mountain**, near Frisco, has a hip and youthful atmosphere. It is snowboard-friendly. With cutting-edge parks and pipe and superior bowls, it is naturally divided into beginner and intermediate areas.

Crested Butte is known as an extreme-ski mecca. The town storic and lively.

BELOW: **Vail** is the nation's largest single-mountain ski and snowboard resort. Vail has vibrant nightlife five-star lodging and dining. It ranks as Colorado's top open-bowl skiing and riding locale.